Ayanna HOWARD

BY STEPHANIE ANNE BOX

ILLUSTRATED B...

Rourke
Educational Media

A Division of
Carson Dellosa Education.

WOMEN IN SCIENCE AND TECHNOLOGY

BEFORE AND DURING READING ACTIVITIES

Before Reading: *Building Background Knowledge and Vocabulary*

Building background knowledge can help children process new information and build upon what they already know. Before reading a book, it is important to tap into what children already know about the topic. This will help them develop their vocabulary and increase their reading comprehension.

Questions and Activities to Build Background Knowledge:

1. Look at the front cover of the book and read the title. What do you think this book will be about?
2. What do you already know about this topic?
3. Take a book walk and skim the pages. Look at the table of contents, photographs, captions, and bold words. Did these text features give you any information or predictions about what you will read in this book?

Vocabulary: *Vocabulary Is Key to Reading Comprehension*

Use the following directions to prompt a conversation about each word.

- Read the vocabulary words.
- What comes to mind when you see each word?
- What do you think each word means?

> ### Vocabulary Words:
> - advanced
> - curious
> - degree
> - engineers
> - innovation
> - persuade
> - robotics
> - software

During Reading: *Reading for Meaning and Understanding*

To achieve deep comprehension of a book, children are encouraged to use close reading strategies. During reading, it is important to have children stop and make connections. These connections result in deeper analysis and understanding of a book.

 ### Close Reading a Text

During reading, have children stop and talk about the following:

- Any confusing parts
- Any unknown words
- Text to text, text to self, text to world connections
- The main idea in each chapter or heading

Encourage children to use context clues to determine the meaning of any unknown words. These strategies will help children learn to analyze the text more thoroughly as they read.

When you are finished reading this book, turn to the next-to-last page for **Text-Dependent Questions** and an **Extension Activity**.

TABLE OF CONTENTS

THE PARTS AND PIECES OF AYANNA

Ayanna Howard grew up in California, in the United States. Both of her parents were **engineers**. They worked together and had their own business. Ayanna's home was always filled with parts from machines such as wires, circuits, and switches. She liked toys that had parts she could build with.

Ayanna was **curious**. She liked to figure out how things worked. Her favorite show was called *The Bionic Woman*. It was about a woman who was part human and part robot. Could that really happen? She dreamed of designing her own Bionic Woman one day.

The Bionic Woman
The show's character was in an accident. She was rebuilt with robot parts. Her robotic arm and legs gave her the power to save people.

CHALLENGES AND SUCCESS

Ayanna liked school. She was good at math and loved numbers. Ayanna was in **advanced** math classes not offered to anyone else her age. Her classmates called her "the smart kid."

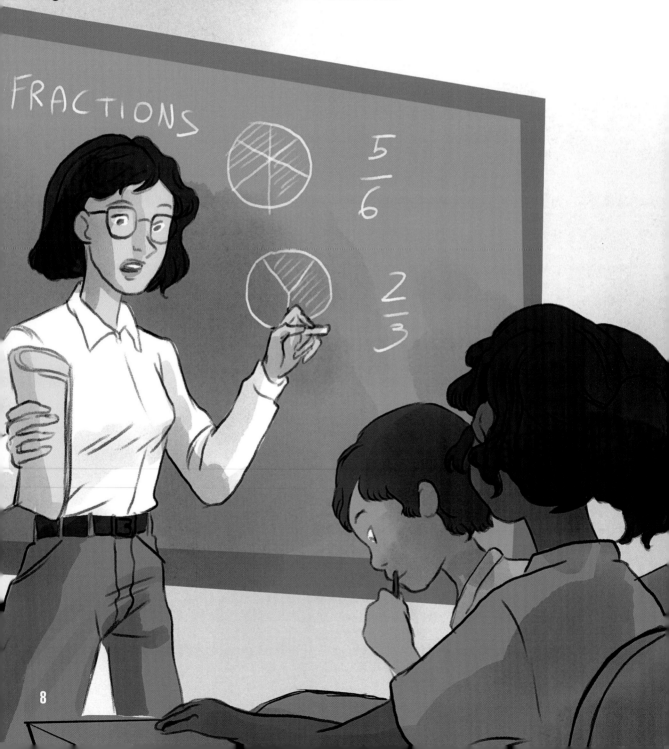

In high school, a teacher urged Ayanna to think about becoming an engineer. She wasn't sure she wanted to be like her parents. Ayanna still had dreams of building a bionic woman.

Ayanna ended up going to college to study engineering. She struggled in her engineering classes but loved her **robotics** classes. At times she doubted her abilities. Her mother reminded her, "Have confidence in yourself. Think about what it is that you have to do in order to compete."

Ayanna never gave up. She graduated from college with a **degree** in engineering. She even went on to get her master's degree and Ph.D. in engineering. She lived by her words, "Don't let anybody persuade you to give up. Know that you are going to experience adversity, but deal with it and keep going in spite of it."

Spending Summers at the Jet Propulsion Lab (JPL)
Ayanna worked at a lab not far from her hometown. She researched things she wondered about. The JPL is a part of the National Aeronautics and Space Administration, or NASA.

BUILDING BIONIC AND BEYOND

Ayanna's dream of building robots came true when she was hired to lead a team of scientists at NASA. Her team would be in charge of making a robot that would be sent to Mars.

They had to make this robot capable of thinking for itself and coming up with solutions to problems it would face.

On her very first day of work at NASA, she noticed an older man was already there. He looked at her and said, "The secretaries aren't here. They moved their meeting down the hall." Ayanna found her courage. She smiled, shook his hand, and introduced herself. She said, "I'm Doctor Ayanna Howard, you're working for me on this project."

Ayanna continued her work at NASA. She helped create **software** for space study. She also helped create drones that flew over glaciers, captured information, and sent back this information. Ayanna was making a difference in the world and beyond.

But she still wanted to make a difference with people. Ayanna moved across the country to Atlanta, Georgia. She became a professor at Georgia Tech. She shared her love of engineering with her students. She learned more about robots.

Ayanna was part of a new project at Georgia Tech. With her team, she created a robot that helped disabled children practice physical therapy while they were at home. With the robots' help, the children could keep getting stronger even when a therapist couldn't be there. Helping children was exciting!

Ayanna knew she was making a difference with children. She felt good about her work. She kept going. Ayanna started her own company called Zyrobotics to share her love of robots with all children.

A Company of Her Own

Zyrobotics provides STEM (Science, Technology, Engineering and Math) learning resources for kids. Ayanna and her team created books, toys, and games to help get young people excited about STEM.

Dr. Ayanna Howard's dream of helping people and the world with robots became a reality. "I'd like to be remembered as someone who changed the world with her research and **innovation**. Someone who changed the world with her wisdom."

TIME LINE

1972: Ayanna Howard was born in Providence, Rhode Island, on January 24.

1974-75: Ayanna's family moved to Altadena, California.

1989: Ayanna graduated from high school in Pasadena, California.

1990: At age 18, Ayanna began an internship with NASA's Jet Propulsion Lab (JPL) and continued working there until after college.

1993: Ayanna graduated with a Bachelor of Science in Engineering from Brown University.

1994: Ayanna graduated with a Master of Science in Electrical Engineering from University of Southern California.

1999: Ayanna graduated with a Ph.D. in Electrical Engineering from University of Southern California and begins full-time job with JPL.

2005: Ayanna graduated with a Master of Business Administration from Claremont Graduate University, and joined the faculty of Georgia Institute of Technology as a professor in Engineering and Robotics.

2010: Ayanna is appointed the chair of the Robotics Ph.D. program at Georgia Tech.

2013: Ayanna Howard founded the technology company, Zyrobotics, which helps students foster a love of STEM awareness.

GLOSSARY

advanced (uhd-VANST): more difficult or demanding

curious (KYOOR-ee-uhs): eager to know or learn about something

degree (di-GREE): a title given to students by a college or university

engineers (en-juh-NEERZ): people trained to design and build machines or structures

innovation (in-uh-VAY-shuhn): a new idea or invention

persuade (pur-SWADE): to make someone do or believe something by giving good reasons

robotics (roh-BAH-tiks): the science of designing, making, and using robots

software (SAWFT-wair): computer programs that control the equipment and tell it what to do

INDEX

TEXT-DEPENDENT QUESTIONS

1. What television show inspired a love of robots for Ayanna?

2. Who encouraged Ayanna to become an engineer?

3. What planet did Ayanna's robot visit?

4. What did the robot Ayanna built for NASA have to be able to do?

5. What is the name of Ayanna's STEM based company?

EXTENSION ACTIVITY

Think about the different kinds of robots that exist today. Robot technology is in cell phones, cars, and vacuums. Think of a task a robot could help you accomplish. What would it do? Explain the benefits of a robot doing that job instead of a person.

ABOUT THE AUTHOR

Stephanie Anne Box is a Kindergarten teacher who loves to sing and learn about history. She lives in Mississippi with her husband, Josh, and spotted dog, Dudley. She is delighted to share her first book with you.

ABOUT THE ILLUSTRATOR

Elena Bia was born in a little town in northern Italy, near the Alps. In her free time, she puts her heart into personal comics. She loves walking on the beach and walking through the woods. For her, flowers are the most beautiful form of life.

© 2021 Rourke Educational Media

www.rourkeeducationalmedia.com

Quote sources: "JPL's Bionic Woman: Dr. Ayanna Howard," NASA, August 8, 2002: https://www.nasa.gov/vision/universe/roboticexplorers/ayanna_howard.html; Meredith Rizzo, Madeline K. Sofia, "Being Different Helped A NASA Roboticist Achieve Her Dream," NPR, December 19, 2017: https://www.npr.org/2017/12/19/569474169/being-different-helped-a-nasa-roboticist-achieve-her-dream; Larry Crowe, "Ayanna Howard," The HistoryMakers TEST ScienceMakers Video Archive, April 15, 2011: http://www.idvl.org/ScienceMakers/iCoreClient.html#/&i=1575

Edited by: Hailey Scragg
Illustrated by: Elena Bia
Interior design by: Alison Tracey

Library of Congress PCN Data

Ayanna Howard / Stephanie Anne Box
(Women in Science and Technology)
 ISBN 978-1-73164-328-5 (hard cover)
 ISBN 978-1-73164-292-9 (soft cover)
 ISBN 978-1-73164-360-5 (e-Book)
 ISBN 978-1-73164-392-6 (ePub)
Library of Congress Control Number: 2020945036

Rourke Educational Media
Printed in the United States of America
01-3502011937